THIS B⬭⬭K BEL⬭NGS T⬭

LET'S PRACTICE WITH THE DOTS FIRST!

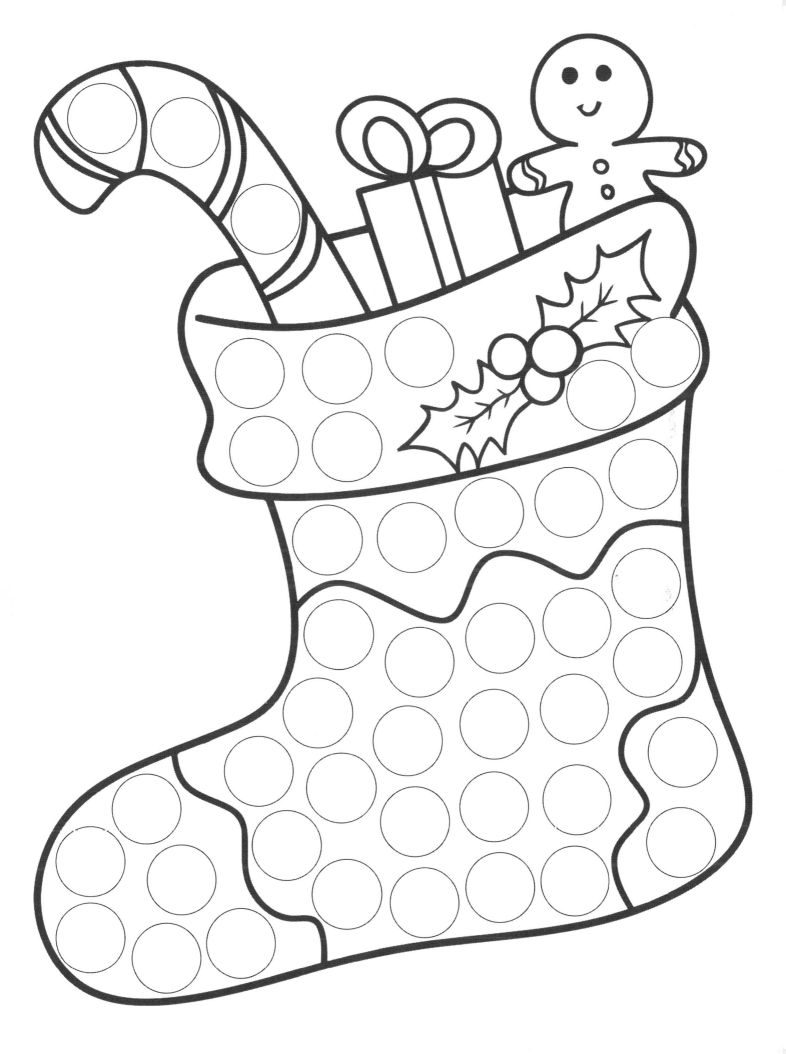

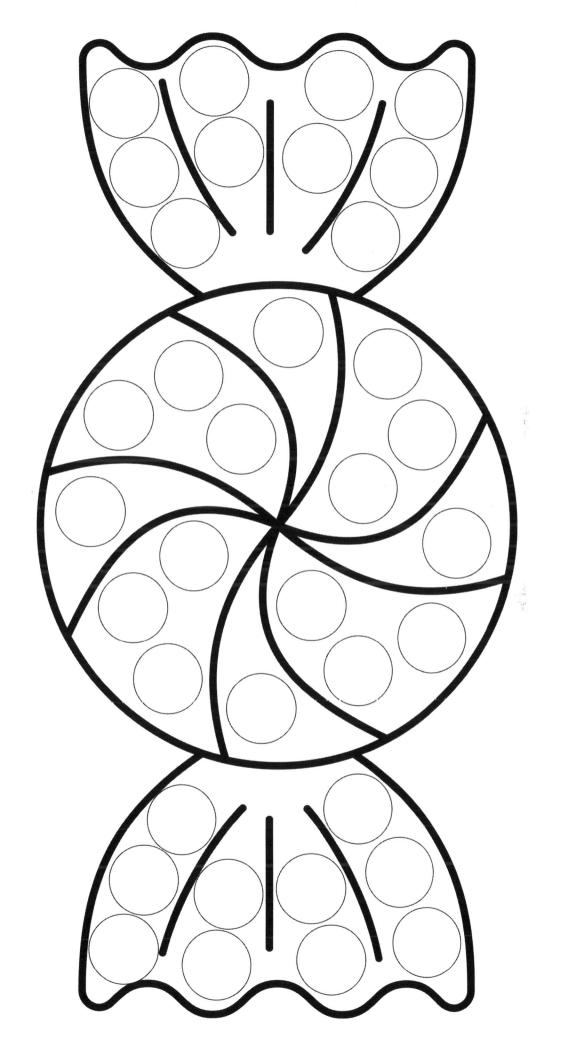

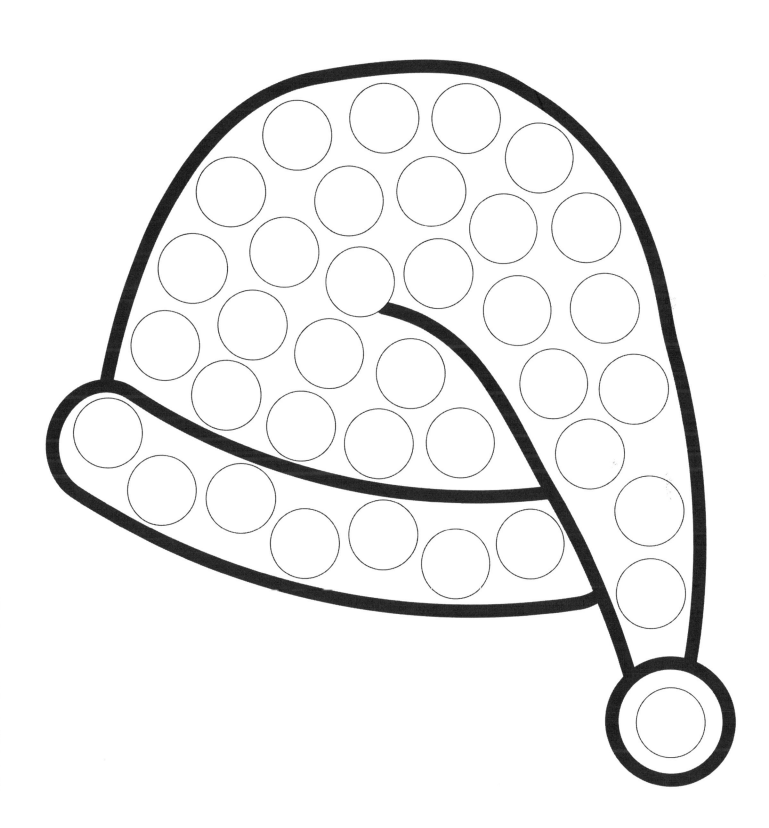

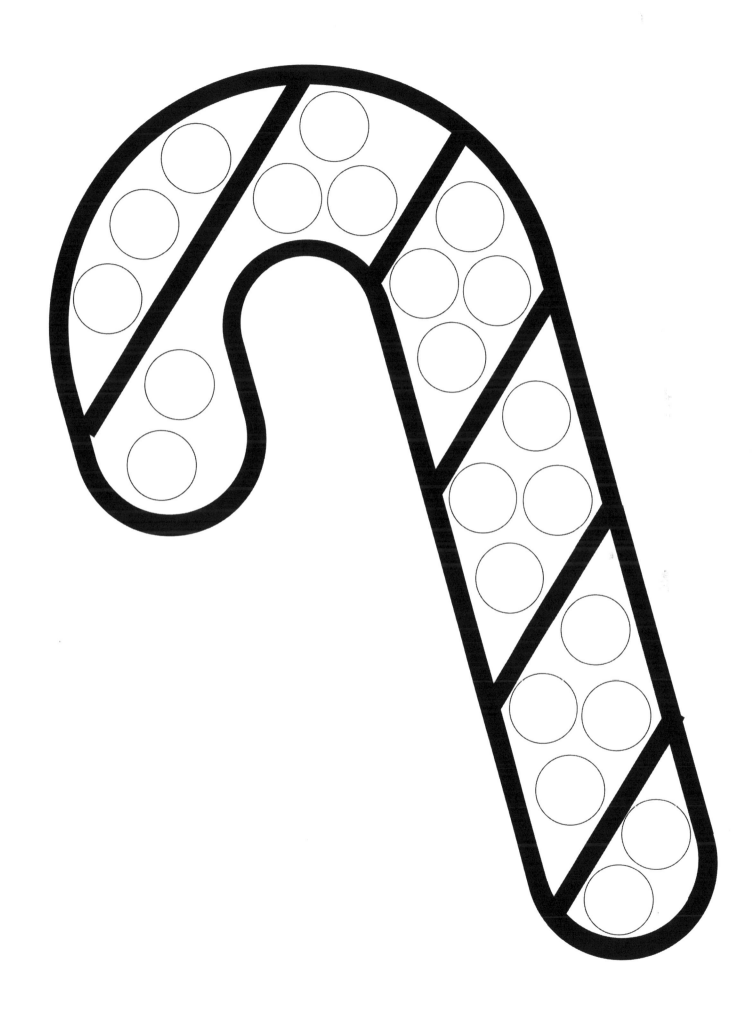

THANK YOU FOR PURCHASING OUR BOOK !

IF YOU LIKE IT, WE WOULD APPRECIATE YOUR REVIEW.

JUST GO TO THE BOOKS AMAZON PAGE AND CLICK ON

"WRITE A CUSTOMER REVIEW"

TO DO THIS YOU CAN ALSO SCAN

THIS QR CODE. IT WILL TAKE NO

MORE THAN 30 SECONDS!

WE VALUE OUR CUSTOMERS AND ALWAYS WELCOME

SUGGESTIONS AND FEEDBACK.

D@ddy and Mummy

Made in the USA
Columbia, SC
09 December 2024